HERMAN®
THE FOURTH TREASURY

Other Popular Herman Books

HERMAN®
THE FOURTH TREASURY

BY JIM UNGER

Andrews, McMeel & Parker
A Universal Press Syndicate Company
Kansas City ● New York

ISBN: 0-8362-2053-6 (paper)
        0-8362-2064-1 (hardbound)
Library of Congress Catalog Card Number: 84-71444

Preface

"Write something for the fourth treasury," they said.
"What about?" I said.
"Talk about humor," they said. *"What makes a joke funny?"*

I think it's possible to understand such things as creativity and humor, or art and even love, if we are able to understand the basic functioning of the human brain. Assuming that we all have a brain in working condition will probably complicate some of my reasoning, but I feel fully justified in calling myself an expert, since I have only the dimmest idea of what I'm talking about anyway.

To keep it simple, the brain has two basic and very different functions. The part I shall call "the mind" is incapable of thought. It absorbs and processes information in a purely logical way to assure survival long before we are smart enough to stick a spoonful of custard in our left ear. Throughout our lives, we are aware of the mind's constant conclusions, but the more intelligent we become, the more we tend to overlook them. We call them names like "hunch," "intuition," or that good old standby, "feelings."

The other part of the brain you know about. It's the part you are most aware of, because it's the part you play with. It's an awful analogy but the two functions could be compared to the front and back wheels of a car. The front wheels are controllable and we give them our full attention whilst driving. The back wheels, although equally important and essential to our progress, are not as interesting, and as long as they keep doing what they always do, we don't give them a great deal of attention.

In the true sense of the word, the mind doesn't actually "think." It simply "works." What makes it so interesting is that it absorbs millions and millions of "bits" of information through at least six senses, most of which bypass our thinking brain to the extent that we are totally unaware of them or their impact.

Young children are not hindered by the self-conscious necessity to do something well. They constantly experiment and allow their minds to solve problems. Having mastered the custard in the ear trick and having that down to a fine art, they try eating an ashtray.

My Uncle Bert once told me, "Every time you fail, you improve." Knowing that this was the same guy who sang the Hallelujah Chorus to his tomato plants, I didn't take him too seriously at the time, but I'm beginning to understand what he meant. Success or failure is irrelevant. As long as the mind receives enough relevant information, it will dispense the best possible solution to the task at hand.

If you hit a golf ball a thousand times in a thousand different directions, the mind would have enough information from all sources to drive the ball straight down the middle of the fairway with the very next swing of the club — provided, and this is the tricky part, you were able to switch off all conscious thoughts and simply focus your mind on the results you wished to achieve.

Have you ever noticed how difficult it is to do something when you think about how you are doing it? I remember my first attempts at meditation after being told to think of nothing else but my breathing. In a few minutes I was gasping for air and totally exhausted.

Another time, appearing on a television show for the first time, I had to walk across a stage in front of three ominous cameras and a live audience. Being frantically aware of what my feet should be doing, I looked like Mae West for the first three steps and dissolved into a wooden Groucho Marx before collapsing into the safety of a blue armchair. As soon as I was seated, I couldn't remember where my hands were supposed to be.

These were all parts of the jigsaw puzzle, and after mulling it over for a while, I resolved that I would strive never to consciously attempt to direct my own mind. Since it was obviously much more adept at breathing and walking than I was, it would be safe to assume that it could handle just about everything else. I imagined my mind saying, "Don't think about what I'm doing. Just tell me what you want and keep sending the postcards."

From all this, I decided never to make decisions. Deciding is just a polite way of saying that we are trying to out-think our minds. If I am faced with a decision, I do nothing. As soon as my mind has been made up, I am filled with an awareness that only one course of action is acceptable and no decision needs to be made.

I'm working my way toward humor. Stay with me.

The human dilemma, in all its forms, is brought about as a result of two realities. Or to be more precise, reality itself and perceived reality. To add to the confusion, almost all of our reality is perceived and our awareness is colored by it throughout our entire lives.

True reality, on the other hand, is like a hole in the ground. It's real enough to fall into and break your neck and can even wreck the suspension on your car. But you can't see it, you can't draw it, and you can't photograph it. It exists not for what it is but for what it isn't. Love is like that too, but I don't want to get confusing.

Anyway, the mind works on reality and perceived reality because it doesn't know the difference and doesn't care. The whole brain functions quite nicely on whatever information it has, and thus we develop our thought patterns and our personality. The problem arises when a more accurate reality enters our thoughts and unbalances our perceptions. It may be met with trauma and doubt and can unleash the whole range of human emotions. Sometimes it can be hilarious. The trick is to leave no doubt. Galileo was locked up not because he said the earth moved around the sun but because his ponderous mathematical explanations left doubts in the minds of others. He should have drawn cartoons.

I told you I'd get to humor.

Imagine paddling in the ocean and seeing a great white shark. If you're like me you would immediately proceed to the center of the nearest major metropolis.

It's worth noting here that a very young child would view the shark with interest and puzzlement. Especially if the child also noticed the rest of us heading for the car park.

It makes the point that the more certain you are about anything, the less you wish to know about it.

As it turns out, this particular shark is a hoax made of inflated rubber. But the fear it generated was as real as it would have been for the real thing. If it floated harmlessly onto the beach, the reality of the situation would have been met with sighs of relief and in some cases hostility. It just wouldn't be all that funny.

But let's imagine that it had moved to within a few feet of the slowest swimmer and suddenly punctured with all the usual turmoil and rude noises of a bursting balloon. It could be hysterically funny to everyone watching, with the possible exception of the sheepish swimmer. And we don't have to concern ourselves with him, because he's Herman.

If I explain what all this has to do with a man walking out of a maternity ward with quadruplets in his arms and complaining that that's the last time he'll use that hospital, there won't be any space left in this book for the cartoons.

Many people ask me if cartoons are art. That's like asking if a baseball player is Babe Ruth. Cartoons are never art but sometimes the drawings are. Drawings and paintings are drawings and paintings. You see them every day in newspapers, magazines, and art stores. Art is different.

Drawings and paintings are produced with varying amounts of skill and dexterity, whereas art is the manifestation of a mind and requires no self-conscious effort.

Strange as it may seem, an artist has to focus his thoughts on reality as he or she perceives it and not on the work. Drawing or painting a tree, an artist is aware of the texture of the wooden bark and the smoothness of the leaves. An artist is aware that a tree doesn't really exist. It's just a group of things that together make up a thing we call a tree. And that brings up the next important point.

Grouping is probably the biggest roadblock to our minds, our art, and our creativity. We are taught to think in groups for easy reference. It's like an old dusty filing system.

I recently helped my young nephew with his homework. He had been given several groups of words and was asked to choose one from each group that didn't belong. One question offered him "dog," "ice cream," and "elephant." He promptly underlined "elephant." When I asked him why, he said because it was the only one that you couldn't get into the back of a car. A few months later, his teacher suggested he might need some extra instruction during the summer break and was only mildly amused when told that he often beats his father at chess. Any kid who can't see the similarity between a small bundle of fur and a five-ton suitcase is going to have a tough time in this world, that's for sure!

If you want to be creative or artistic, forget groups. Incidentally, that includes race, nationality, religion, politics, and football teams. Whatever else it does it will make you a lot happier; and that's what this book is all about anyway.

One of my favorite quotations came from a Zen philosopher many, many years ago. He wrote, "Painting a beautiful picture is simple. First become a beautiful person, then paint naturally."

I sincerely believe that there is a natural beauty in all of us, buried beneath misconception and self-conscious awareness. Naturalness unmolested is always beautiful, just as art is always beautiful.

Whether we are sixteen or sixty, it's a strange irony that the more natural we are, the more attractive we are to others. Sadly, we are very often led to believe the exact opposite.

Love is blind because it lives in that part of the brain that is beyond the reach and control of thoughts. You can't think you love; you know it.

Thoughts and senses provide all the information, but only the mind can love, just as only the mind can fear. This being so, our minds often feel alone and lost in the universe and are quick to find comfort in the naturalness of others. When we catch a glimpse of true nature, we rejoice in it because we see ourselves in the naturalness of others and realize we are amongst friends.

When I draw Herman, I draw funny-looking people, saying and doing very natural things. I know why you laugh and I think you know why you laugh. It may be a comfort to you to know that millions of other people around the world are laughing too. It's certainly a comfort to me. I was beginning to think I was on the wrong planet.

I hope this book makes you happy.

—JIM UNGER

**"What was that cyclist
shouting about back there?"**

"Aw c'mon doc, let me
borrow a mirror."

"I can't seem to make up
my mind about this one!"

"Where are you hopping off to?"

"If anyone needs me, Joyce,
I'll be up on the roof
for about 20 minutes."

"Is it ten minutes to five already?"

"Quick, put it on.
Someone's coming!"

"They don't allow those
on my planet."

"I'll have a coffee and
a Danish to go."

"As I wasn't too busy, I made you my international award-winning hamburger-deluxe."

"I don't mind you reading over my shoulder, but don't do the crossword puzzle."

"Look, you're 103 years old, you've got to start taking better care of yourself."

"Your honor, before the jury retires to reach a verdict my client wishes to present each of them with a little gift of jewelry."

"Have you got a 24-slice toaster?"

"Dad, a guy at school said
we all came from humans."

"If you're so smart, how come the world
was in such a mess before I got here?"

"You'd better remove your make-up.
I've got some good news."

"I don't mind the 17th floor
as long as I have 64 sheets."

"What did you *expect*
to find in oxtail soup?"

"Will you keep the noise down! We're
trying to have a party next door."

"Can you change a $100 bill?"

MATERNITY

"Whad'dyer mean triplets!
He was here first."

"I hate bothering you, but my wife wants to
know if she passed her driver's test."

LIFE GUARD

"I hope you know your stuff.
I'm a very weak swimmer."

"I'll have to X-ray your arm again.
This one is overexposed."

"D'you mind if I take a photo? It's not often we get a 15-cent tip."

"Haven't you got one in English?"

"I hear you're looking for an aggressive salesman."

"I can't eat anymore of these turquoise peas!"

"Now I suppose you're gonna sulk because I wouldn't give you the afternoon off!"

"You're the one who kept telling me you were a 'go-getter.'"

"Simpson, bring me an order of onion rings and move that candle further down the table."

"That was my ex-boyfriend's car!"

"Is it too tight across the shoulders?"

"I can't understand anyone being afraid of dogs."

"I'll have a cheeseburger and a root beer."

"Welcome to planet earth. Is your mother home?"

"It's a pity you're unemployed! You need a couple of weeks off work."

"I lost the key for my padlock!"

"I wonder why they make these finger bandages so long?"

"I told you not to eat popcorn while you've got hiccups."

"Here's one you'll love! Two weeks in an open boat without food and water."

"I know it's your birthday soon, but what can I buy a woman who has everything?"

"He's only been at his company for a year and already he's getting the minimum wage!"

"As soon as he's finished, rush that glass of water over to table nine."

"Is the war over?"

"All the cups are dirty. D'you
want your coffee in that?"

"Be careful with the wine. I had
trouble getting the cork out."

"Take that back! It tastes like
the stuff my wife makes."

"Got a dog to fit that?"

"Your friend Muriel is going
through Harry's pockets again!"

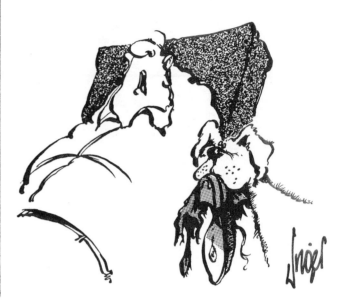

"The mailman's been!"

"Whoever shouted 'Turkey' was correct."

"Now scrape that off the carpet and
serve it to him on a clean plate."

"Remember your blood pressure!"

"Of course it's half eaten! You said
you wanted the chef's salad."

"I was wondering how
you'd play that shot."

"Ignorance of the law
is no excuse, buddy!"

"How am I supposed to know you're allergic to these if you don't tell me!"

"If you can spare the time, Williams, I'd like to see you in my office."

"Gimme 14 hot dogs."

"Was he as short as that in real life?"

"So this is Dotty, your wife."

"In your case, we have no interest at all!"

"Cindy's getting a job at a bank and needs you as a reference."

"There's four billion of them down here! Make sure none get on the ship before we take off."

"Guy in the front row wants to know if you like blueberry or custard cream?"

"Coffee is 50 cents for the first half-hour and 30 cents for each additional half-hour."

"The top keeps flying off the food mixer."

"That robot that replaced you at work has been laid off!"

"I like the color but won't the water keep running out?"

"I think that dark shadow is where I spilled some coffee."

"Can you cut me a star-shaped piece of glass to fit that hole?"

"You're supposed to read it aloud!"

"Nurse . . . see if you can find my little rubber hammer."

"Have you got any old bricks I can take to my karate lesson?"

"He wasn't always bald. It's acid rain."

"I asked him what he wanted for our anniversary and he said 'two minutes of silence'."

"The doctor thinks he's going to be very musical."

"Okay, you've got the job!
On your mark, get set, . . ."

"I think we've decided on the
ruby-and-diamond cluster."

"Oh, Herman! You're my
very first husband."

"Where did you put my
book on archaeology?"

"George, how many years have I been coming in this candy store?"

"This wildlife book you sold me is nothing but animals!"

"I told you last week I had to work late tonight!"

"I don't really want a diagnosis. What diseases have you got for under $50?"

"This is your loan application back from our head office."

"204 pounds on the left and 189 pounds on the right."

"Look at that! 62 years old and not a single cavity."

"The TV keeps switching back to 'Wild Kingdom'!"

"I'm your new secretary. Am I an
hour late or 23 hours early?"

"I need a dishwasher that can handle heavy, baked-on grease — three times a day."

"Here . . . tell your mother we're out. She won't believe me."

"You had a hair transplant?"

"You won't find a job in the sports section!"

"This rascal chased the wife's
mother 20 feet up a tree."

"You say you were inside robbing
the bank and someone stole your car?"

"You wouldn't even have that job if
my Grandpa hadn't got the flu."

"Mother sent us each a Christmas card."

44

"They dropped the speeding charge but I've got to pay for the three storefronts and the railway station."

"Here, work your way through that lot and I'll go easy on you next year."

"Fourteen shopping minutes to Christmas!"

"This your idea of a good old-fashioned Christmas — turkey pizza?"

"If I didn't love you I wouldn't eat *this,* would I?"

"I've been at the hospital all day. My wife broke her fist."

"I knew he was really sick. He hasn't complained about anything for three days."

"She tries to watch what she eats but her eyes aren't quick enough."

"We've been happily married for
two years — 1938 and 1945."

"I'll take another bottle
of this after-shave."

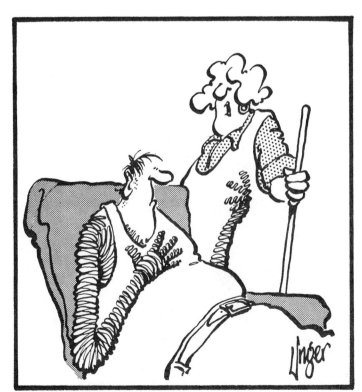

"I told you not to lay in
the bath all afternoon!"

"That's the last time we'll
use this hospital!"

"He wants to give us $1,000 to
use the moon for a few days!"

"When are you going to face the fact
that you're a lousy pickpocket?"

"That's $194.32, less four
cents for the bonus coupon."

"We were just toying with the
idea of going to see a movie. Can
you come back in about three minutes?"

"This is a much bigger apartment than we're used to."

"Are we still hiring minorities?"

"I sold half the business!"

"I don't care if it *is* his birthday!"

"The judge gave my lawyer five years
before he even got around to me!"

"Your honor, my client is the
product of a broken home."

"The guy across the street wants
to know what you're cooking."

"Whaddyer mean, 'The strawberries aren't fresh'? I just opened the can five minutes ago!"

HERMAN
by JIM UNGER.

WHAT'S THE WORD?

IT'S ALL SET...I'M GOING OVER THE WALL AT MIDNIGHT.

MAKE SURE YOU REMEMBER EVERYTHING.

DON'T WORRY. I'VE GOT IT ALL WRITTEN DOWN.

YOU'D BETTER GO OVER IT ONE LAST TIME...

TWO HUNDRED AND SEVEN CHEESEBURGERS...EIGHTY-NINE HOT-DOGS...AND ONE HUNDRED AND NINETY-TWO FRIES.

53

"How long have you been
on the night shift!"

"If I get a good mark, you could be looking
at a very nice apple tomorrow morning."

"It's my new slimming book."

"Can't you hum something else?"

"I can't hear the peasants singing. You'd better put the guard on 'red alert.'"

"Come on! Tell him you're sorry for stepping on him at the top of the stairs."

"We can't stand here all day. It must have jammed."

"I'm sorry, we're out of 'Multivitamins Plus Iron.'"

"Ralph, what's the price
on these lizards' feet?"

"I'll skip the dessert menu. I don't
like to run on a full stomach."

"Your honor, my client thinks
ten years is a little harsh and requests
permission to approach the bench."

"I won't be home Friday.
They've changed all the locks."

"Up and left."

"I'm having a fabulous evening, but I really must be home by 8 o'clock."

"385 pounds, including the towel."

"I knew we shouldn't have bought waterfront property!"

"Do you have such a thing as a refrigerator with a revolving door?"

"For the last time: I do not want today's special."

"In 35 years, you're my first case of this!"

"I think we had much nicer diseases when I was a girl."

"I've found a secret room!"

"This is the last one he painted."

"I'd ask you in, but I've only got one chair."

"Is that the man who tried to mug you?"

"Nurse, you'd better put these on."

"I see for the last 15 years you've been in financial management."

"Make sure he's home by 4 o'clock."

"She's here to get some entry forms for the Miss Universe competition."

"You can sit there 'til I find out where you hid my glasses!"

"I've never told anyone before,
but I was aiming at a crocodile."

"We were wondering if we could extend the
maximum limit on our charge account?"

"As soon as we got married I realized
two can live as cheaply as six."

"Can't you help me catch the canary?"

"You're looking at the next general manager of 'Louie's Takeout Pizza.'"

"I just seem to be walking around in circles all day!"

"Old George has been with the company 38 years. Do I hear $300?"

"My daughter tells me you're hoping for a career in shipping."

"He jumped over 15½ buses!"

"He wants to sit with his back to the wall."

"Some of the guys at work are coming over
this evening to help me do the dishes."

"Can't you take a joke?"

"It's part of our new policy
of 'preventive surgery.'"

"He seems to have decided on
a baseball scholarship."

"You wanna have good eyesight
if you go abroad, don't you?"

"Just give him your money, dear. The last
one sued us for the medical bills."

"Be careful how you try that one on, Madame. This is a very old building."

"She kept saying the dance floor was lumpy."

"I think you'll find my test results are a pretty good indication of your abilities as a teacher."

"Let me know immediately if you start feeling the urge to move sideways."

67

"I want you to take one of these
with water every four years."

"We were finding it very
hot in here, Warden."

"He's a bit nervous."

"Here's a nice shady spot over here!"

"Are you the guy who advertised
he'd found a wallet?"

"A whole boiled egg! So two years
of night school finally paid off."

"I think my memory's coming back! Ask me
who won the World Series in 1998."

"As you can see, your insurance
doesn't cover 'family squabbles.'"

"Arnold, will you please stand away from that on-off switch?"

"I was halfway across the freeway and my hat blew off."

"I've lost the key!"

"He said he shot it in the desert."

"Did Grandpa give you permission to take that off his bad leg?"

"Remember Ralphy, the moron?
He's making $250,000 a year."

"Just relax and get your memory
back. Don't lay there worrying
about that $8 you owe me."

"Got a room with a panoramic
view of the city?"

"I lost track of my age years ago,
but I think I'm about 22."

"As we'll be flying over water, we present the following demonstration of what to do in the case of shark attack."

"I'd say that was just about a total eclipse, wouldn't you?"

"And for the man who has everything, we have this personal nuclear deterrent."

"My wife would like to look at some fur coats. Got any binoculars?"

"This says you have a tendency to grovel."

"Did you or did you not tell him I was a Homo sapiens?"

"Lily, run upstairs and see if this guy's gas barbecue is in our bedroom."

"I guess I'll plead not guilty just to get the old ball rolling."

"I had over 200 hours of flying
time when I was your age."

"I know it's probably uncomfortable,
but we need them as evidence."

"Forgot the cat's birthday, didn't you?"

"I thought I said those flying fish had
to be back in their bowl by 8 o'clock!"

"Mrs. Baxter, I don't think things are going to work out."

"Of course, we're looking for a man who can work without supervision."

"When was this passport photo taken?"

"Get that lab on the phone. This chest X-ray only shows the top of his head!"

"OK, don't start showing off!"

"I finally found his credit cards, taped inside the TV cabinet."

"Mildew, can you work an hour's overtime tonight?"

"I see the old dollar's taken another beating."

"Whoever heard of anyone studying
for an eye examination!"

"Quick, drink this! It'll
settle your stomach."

"Will you keep your head still!"

"Your brother-in-law is
marooned on a desert island."

"D'you buy used cats?"

"Her mother had a coat made and put 'squirrel' on the endangered species list!"

"I ordered a coffee when I came in. Do you think you could give me a progress report when the beans leave South America?"

"You need plenty of rest. You'd better stay in the gutter for a few days."

"I left the circus 17 years ago and I think I still miss it!"

"Take off your tie and unbutton your shirt. There are nine women on the jury."

"I'm sure he couldn't have done it intentionally!"

"You were a stronger man on our first honeymoon."

"I've got a stabbing pain in my left kidney."

"Of the smaller breeds, these are about the best guard dogs."

"Your boss didn't want you to lay here worrying about the work piling up, so he fired you."

"Breathe deeply and take a quick look at my bill."

"Open up! I want to take a look down your throat."

"You'd be surprised if you knew how many people walk out without paying!"

"You were going to fix the screen door six months ago!"

"The only time he's got a 48-inch chest is when he stands on his head!"

"Don't keep saying 'I do.' You're the best man."

"Separate checks, please."

"Your teeth are fantastic, but your gums have to come out."

"Er, hello! Your daughter's husband has been called away on business for three months."

"Hey, Pierre! D'you want half of this apple?"

"This is Dr. Elgin, our expert
on tropical diseases."

"You shouted it LAST time!"

"Unless I'm mistaken, you had a
pretty hefty pay hike in 1967."

"Hey, Lily! Was it 1958 I got my bronze medal for the 'foxtrot'?"

"This should hold it!"

"Anything under $25,000 nowadays is considered 'junk jewelry.'"

"I need to borrow your 68 cents 'mad money.'"

"Here, take this, but make sure you get home in 90 seconds."

"Your honor, a 25-year jail sentence would jeopardize my client's job at the supermarket."

"I'm sorry, sir, visiting hours *are* over."

"Put your stupid hands down: He's looking for the dentist."

"Make sure he pays cash."

"Here's the menu. I'll be back in a couple of hours."

"You can stop waving goodbye. I'm staying!"

"Is it still half-price for kids?"

"We need a six-foot ladder and an eight-foot ladder."

"Table for three."

"Is this the guy who was stuck
in the elevator for three days?"

"Can I go in first? This is a real emergency."

"Got any nice gift-wrapping paper?"

"I want you to walk two miles a day
. . . and take my dog with you."

"I'm sorry, I haven't laughed
like this for months."

"You've got the job. Now, take
these home and practice kissing them."

"We went on strike last week and
they brought in scab convicts."

"I hope you had a radio
transmitter on that ball!"

"I'm sorry! He's taking karate lessons."

"This is not an illegal strike. We're
having a 72-hour lunch break."

"You should never use an electric
blanket on a waterbed!"

"D'you know how many people are
hit by lightning every year?"

"We ate at home, so we just want
to check how much we saved."

"D'you have any other references apart
from this one from your mother?"

"Grandma just made a tidy profit on
some of your old report cards."

"This is new. . . . 'mega-puncture.'"

"I don't know who he is! He was there when I woke up this morning."

"One minute, 52 seconds. I could have died of thirst!"

"I think I'm gonna get the job. Call me back in five minutes."

"Oh, no! Somebody's broken
the bedroom window."

"We're on our second honeymoon. Make
sure our rooms are not too close together."

"The guy at the pet store said
he needs more exercise."

"You're a little underweight.
Put this in your pocket."

**"How many times have I told you not
to put your feet on the table?"**

"I gave up two hours of sleep
to apply for this job!"

"She gave me a box of chocolates
for my birthday with 11 missing."

"You sat up in the middle of the night
and shouted, 'Rub two sticks together.'"

"Dad, I'm writing my life story.
Is 'poverty-stricken' one word?"

"Can we borrow your coat?
We're going to the movies."

"A vote for me is a vote
for the small businessman."

"I take it your business
meeting was a success."

"Wilson, don't drag your
nails down the blackboard."

"It's got a two-level finished basement."

"Here we go! Step one: Take off your shirt."

"Oh no! He's bought a trampoline."

"OK, that's enough for one day.
I'll see you next Tuesday."

"Can you stand on your right leg?"

"Marriage is give and take. I eat your cooking so *you* do the dishes."

"You can earn $504 a week if you work the full 168 hours."

"These are for you in court. We're going for 'insanity'."

"Don't let George scare you.
He's in for art forgery."

"We need something fast
for about 10 minutes."

"Stay away from those wooden ones.
I nearly got my head blown off!"

"You'd better hurry up and decide.
The warranty runs out in 15 minutes."

"It's not my fault if my dad
won't lend me the car!"

"D'you still want 'the catch of the day'?"

"If I'm not back in 20
minutes, get a divorce."

"He wants another 50 bucks . . .
pair of nines and a queen."

"Why don't you save the money and
put it toward plastic surgery?"

"It's been six days. Has he
reported me missing yet?"

"I'm sorry, Wilson. After 16
years of loyal service, you're
being replaced by this microchip."

"Did you say on the phone you were
'in the 20s' or 'born in the '20s'?"

"And now for a look at the latest picture from a weather satellite."

"People are beginning to complain about too much violence on cave walls."

"It's not catching, is it?"

"Fish and chips and 42 chef's salads."

"I told you it was supposed
to go around your neck."

HERMAN by JIM UNGER

THE CRYSTAL BALL NEVER LIES.

I SEE YOU TAKING A PLANE TRIP IN THE VERY NEAR FUTURE...

YOU'RE RIGHT!

YOU JUST BOUGHT SOME NEW, EXPENSIVE, LIGHTWEIGHT LUGGAGE.

RIGHT AGAIN!

I SEE IT COVERED IN DUST AND SURROUNDED BY A LOAD OF CAMELS.

I'M FLYING TO CHICAGO!

YOUR BAGS ARE GOING TO ISTANBUL.

"Why don't you wait until
you're both working?"

"If you insist on laughing, sir, I must
ask you to browse in the humor section."

"I'll have to deduct five points
for cornering on two wheels."

"It says, 'Your day will be greatly
influenced by the planet Neptune.'"

"So I'm half an hour late! So what?"

"I married her for her looks and she married me for my money. . . . Now we're even."

"He's back again!"

"Hang on, there's a guy here complaining about the bus being overcrowded."

"I'll be back in an hour, Muriel."

"Got any more of those blue-and-white striped ones that taste like tuna?"

"For the last time, Randolph, I'm the best man and you're the groom. We can't change places!"

"Come on. You were all excited when you saw it on TV."

"I know you're three weeks away from retirement, but it's either fire you now or fork out for a gold watch."

"I used to have a bigger eye chart but I wasn't making any money."

"They're $12 . . . but don't worry, I'll keep them in a vault and wear an imitation."

"I've seen it before. He's changing into a butterfly."

"Well, nobody can say you didn't try."

"Old Rex has been in the family for as far back as I can remember."

"You're getting overheated. Go outside in the fresh air and clean the windows."

"I can't help you if you're just going to sit there mooing."

"You haven't eaten your chicken!"

"You got any idea how
fast you were going?"

"Nothing on?"

"This isn't the right water
pump, but I'll make it fit."

"Just cut off a dollar's worth."

"If it's for your wife, sir,
I'd suggest crushed velvet."

"Get a move on. The tranquilizer
dart's wearing off."

"My stomach's having a tough time
getting used to well-cooked food."

"I'm sorry, sir, that's not hand luggage."

"What's so dumb about cutting out
a full-page advertisement?"

"Let go, sweetheart, and Mommy
will give you this bone."

"How can I find anything when you keep
leaving this razor all over the bathroom?"

"He's out! Can I take a message?"

"How was I supposed to
know it fired torpedoes?"

"Is your wife still taking singing lessons?"

"He wants me to tell you that
the pills aren't working."

"This guy wants to borrow
your long ladder."

"I thought you said you
were an airline pilot."

"How come my sister gets big blue
capsules and I get cough syrup?"

"Table for two . . . name of 'Kong.'"

"Come on, Herbert. The gates
open in five minutes."

"Forty words per minute
doesn't include spelling."

"You certainly have a way with animals."

"Give me your credit card. I'm
getting these for your birthday."

"I hope you like bamboo soup."

"No, sir. This is not a Greek restaurant.
You have the menu upside down."

"I had to make a videotape of myself
telling him his supper's ready."

"OK, you've got the job. But
you make sure you have a big
breakfast before coming to work."

"C'mon, Dave! I saw him first."

"We've decided on a small
wedding. I'm not going."

"I'm putting you down as
'potential donor material.'"

"I bet you didn't remember that this is the same coffee shop where we met 25 years ago."

"George . . . Have we got 900 rolls of this 'imitation stone'?"

"Get a move on! She'll be home in 10 minutes."

"I'm—fine—how—are—you?"

"He's probably taking a
breather on his way north."

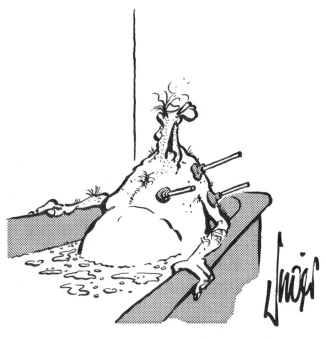

"Will you please speak to those kids."

"Did you have your hair done at
that new place on Market Street?"

"I just hope that's not the
water you had your teeth in!"

"We had to remove your brain for a couple of days, so just try to relax."

"I gotta open you up again.
Those things are $36 a pair!"

"Listen, Ron, I'm not
going bowling tonight."

"Something just landed on my back!"

INFORMATION

"I suppose you heard about that
blonde who used to work at the bank."

"Now don't hit Grandad's foot."

"If he had six wives, how come there was no Henry the Ninth?"

"They hung this mirror upside down."

"Get back in bed!!!"

"I brought him over because
I want him to apologize."

"I'm sorry. What more can I say!"

"We got a nice postcard from those
little green guys in the UFO."

"He doesn't have a diploma, but
he does have carpentry experience."

"You should stay off that left
foot for a couple of days."

"She said if I don't finish the
fence in time, I won't be able
to go to her sister's wedding."

"Which parent do you want to sign it: my
natural father, my stepfather, my mother's
third husband, my real mother or my natural
father's fourth wife who lives with us?"

"The computer says it'll probably try
to stick that rubber thing in your mouth."

"Is it true you like your employees to speak their minds, big nose?"

"The doctor said you can come home on Friday if I get rid of the cat."

"How d'you expect people to read labels that are stuck on upside down?"

"It shot over there, under the stove!"

"What do you mean, you don't recognize this court?"

"Rub this on your feet three times a day, during meals."

"Take two just before you go to bed and two just before you wake up."

"She wants six chicken wings.
Three left and three right."

"You've broken my best flowerpot!"

"Just out of idle curiosity, how d'you
manage to serve leftovers 14 days in a row?"

"And just where have you been
at 3 o'clock in the morning?"

"Mr. White is here for his annual checkup, doctor."

"So much for your theory
that the earth is round."

"I'm starting my vacation tomorrow,
so I'll leave you 14 newspapers."

"Port ... starboard ... port ... starboard.
Can't you speak English?"

"How do you spell 'escapologist'?"

"When I was your age, I could do the 100-yard dash in 12 minutes!"

"Hello, Frank. Does my insurance cover me for snapped off needles?"

"What exactly do you mean, Doc, by 'your blood pressure pills aren't working'?"

"Do you have any other hobbies besides 'birdwatching'?"

"One egg sandwich with live
entertainment, $12.50."

"I do have your size, madame, but
you'll have to buy the table with it."

"Stale doughnut and a cup
of cold coffee, Harry."

"Today's special is
spaghetti and meatballs."

"Hey, stewardess. Run through that seatbelt demonstration a few more times. It's unbelievably tricky!"

"Mention something about her not fooling around with my stereo equipment."

"Dad took us to Sea World and fell in."

"Will you get a move on with those loafers? He's trying to leave."

"Solid as a rock and light as a feather."

"Well, you knew we had only
one tree when you bought it."

"If you want to leave, Maxine,
I won't stand in your way."

"When are you gonna start facing reality?"

"You say you spent five
years at the North Pole?"

"Don't look like that. You'll be boasting
about this for the rest of your life."

"I hear your husband is a ventriloquist."

"According to this, we gave a
45-year-old woman a skin rash."

"Did you happen to notice which chicken?"

"It never ceases to amaze
me what people throw away."

"Wilson, I'm beginning to have
serious doubts about your
abilities as a bookkeeper."

"This is your last chance.
Turn that stereo down."

"Will you quit screaming!
I'm cleaning my glasses!"

"I don't normally buy bug spray at the door,
but the one I use obviously doesn't work."

"Er . . . stay cool, baby . . .
and, er . . . what's happening?"

"I've worn a 34-inch waist
ever since I was a teen-ager."

"Did you tell the cat he
could have my striped shirt?"

HERMAN by JIM UNGER

WHAT'S HAPPENING, SID?

YOU KNOW, SIDNEY, I'VE BEEN SITTING HERE THINKING...
...TWO THOUSAND PEOPLE PER DAY LOOK THROUGH THOSE BARS.....

AT THREE BUCKS A PIECE..
...THAT'S SIX GRAND..
...EACH AND EVERY DAY!

FORTY THOUSAND A WEEK... WITH EARLY CLOSING ON SUNDAYS.

OVER TWO MILLION A YEAR...
EXCLUDING THE GIFT SHOP.

...AND THEY GIVE ME A LOUSY 'RETREAD'!

"The changing room is occupied.
Crouch down behind the tie rack."

"Some florist delivered a bunch
of flowers here by mistake."

"Lily, see if there's anything
on the 6 o'clock news about it."

"A spot of car trouble, officer. My
chauffeur's gone for a tow truck."

"You're an hour late! Don't blame me
if your cheese sandwich is ruined."

"The doctor says he's got
to get plenty of rest."

"Don't you ever get nervous,
living 50 floors up?"

"Your birthday gift is in the garage,
charging up my car battery."

"I didn't ask you if you smoked. I said, 'Do you need any matches?'"

"Not him!"

"My goodness! It says in another month, I'll be charging $20 a visit."

"What are you doing now? Throw the Frisbee."

"Wagstaff, these experiments
have got to stop."

"I spoke to the doctor. He said
you're taking too much iron."

"It's the first time he's played
with the Boston Symphony."

"So anyway, I thought, you won't be back
for 10 minutes. I'll grab a hot dog."

"You'll be pleased to know, madame, we just landed safely at the international airport."

"Now let's see. You say yours has three little blue dots on it."

"I got her in a poker game. I had a pair of eights and the other guy had three jacks."

"Dad burst six balloons with one dart."

"Obviously you weren't at the meeting this morning."

"Couldn't you find yourself a nice boyfriend from this planet?"

"Dear Pinkie: Having a wonderful time in the south of France."

"Quick! Your mother sent me a birthday present. Get a bucket of water."

"D for Donny, E for Elvis, A for Abba and R for Rolling Stones."

"Joyce, give this guy a second cup of coffee. He found my car keys."

"I hear you're giving a series of lectures on body-building."

"Every major problem on this planet can be linked to overcrowding."

"Keep your head down, Billy-Joe."

"I'll have your red snapper, white potatoes and green beans. D'you have any blue carrots?"

"Hey, Lily. You were in the army. What's an 'adjective'?"

"Well, I sure wasn't making any money as a pet store."

"I'd like to see a set of your unbreakable dishes."

"What really bugs me is I
can't remember what I did."

"We usually put 30 percent on!"

"Dougie, have we got these in coral pink?"

"I'm planning a solo voyage around
the world. D'you want to come?"

"You're not staying home from work. It's payday."

"Cost me $60 and she only wore it twice."

"I'm making you Dobson's personal assistant until his feet get better."

"Mrs. Rodriguez, next Monday I want you to stand in for me at the annual stockholders meeting."

"I've only got a few minutes.
Where are the short stories?"

"I called your receptionist this
morning for a 3 o'clock appointment
to have my eyes tested."

"These won't help you sleep, but they'll
stop you tossing and turning all night."

"You're like my brother-in-law.
He's got short arms."

"You'd be in a lousy mood, too, if you had
to deal with twits like this every day."

"Hello, operator. I wanna place
a collect call to the zoo."

"Keep moving your feet around. I don't
want these vegetables to stick."

"I'm not nagging. I just said I hope you're not going to ruin my sister's wedding."

"Why would I take your pipe? Have you looked in the kitchen?"

"Thank you, Burrows, for that descriptive insight into the nuclear arms race."

"Very impressive. How do you feel about relocating?"

"Nice job, Percy. See you next time."

"Does that say, 'Learn to read in seven days'?"

"Detective Parker, zoo patrol."

"I can't find his file. Is it under 'C' for crazy or 'H' for horse?"

"What's it gonna be: go for walkies, or have this bone and watch the game on TV?"

"Good grief, man. It's only a parking ticket!"

"Take up the slack."

"Dad, where can we go to burn some crops?"

"Think back . . . two years ago
. . . you sold me a gerbil."

"I see you finally fixed
the crack in the wall."

"I got 30 days with no parole, Mildred.
Don't waste your life. Find someone else."

"I explained the risks to his wife and
she thinks we should go for it."

"You have my word of honor,
it is only a rabies shot."

"We're closing in five minutes.
I'll get you a blanket."

"It's a little round white
thing, comes out of a chicken."

"Eat this school report
and let me do the talking."

"They took away all my mink coats and
my diamond-encrusted wristwatch."

"I could literally double my
income with a 20-foot ladder."

"I need one more gallon
of that ceiling white."

"My cousin, Herbie, got a job at the zoo."

"I think we can dispense with hand signals
in the middle of the Pacific Ocean."

"Got any room in your freezer?"

"Who told you you could
take it out yourself?"

"Somebody tell that new assistant
manager I found his sport jacket."

"I didn't bring my glasses. Does that say you've been pardoned?"

"Just answer me yes or no, sir. Were you or were you not the only employee who knew the combination?"

"Is there such a thing as a bathroom scale fitted with shock absorbers?"

"I've come to ask for your daughter's hand in moving my furniture."

"Here's the latest word on that mystery object seen over our city this evening."

"A message from your grandson, sir."

"You look like a man with the minimum daily requirement of intelligence. Where can I find a book on self-confidence?"

"I think the highlight of my professional career is knowing I helped someone like you."

"Whaddyer mean you don't know
what it is? Who cooked it?"

"The computer handles
all our applications."

"I told you to get size 10."

"Is that what they teach you
at mailman's college?"

"Can't you see I'm eating? Why don't you push off and go look at the penguins?"

"Detective Shenko, lady. You called in about a missing cat . . ."

"Randolph! Your blind date is here."

"What about monkeys? You must have monkeys!"

"I liked the way you kicked that tire. Very few of these young kids today understand the finer points of a quality vehicle."

"See if you can get a saber-toothed tiger for the weekend. And make sure it's not all fat."

"I told you you'd love it."

"I wish I could lay around in bed all day every time I had a sore throat."

"I'll be honest with you, this is not the largest planet in the universe."

"When we get home, pretend you're out of breath."

"Is that 'turkey with noodles,' 'beef with cabbage' or 'lasagna'?"

"Let's see. . . . Your wife had a baby girl at 2:15 a.m., a boy at 2:20 a.m. and another two girls at 2:25 a.m."

"Who said 'No man is an island'?"

"I think this one is yours."

"They all want coffee."

"We're living in very
strange times, Martha."

"Don't touch that volume control."

"Imagine them wanting
a $5 delivery charge!"

"Clamp!"

"I think you'll enjoy working
here. We're very informal."

"Have you got one with an eye-level grill?"

"OK. Here he comes. Now remember everything I taught you."

"I'm back!"

"Your four years' hard work in the basement just came waltzing up the stairs."

"My daughter tells me you're a lifeguard."

"Personally, I think it's all these chemicals they spray on the fruit."

"The housewarming party has been postponed."

"Any questions so far?"

"Mildew, I'm not accusing you,
but there's a grape missing."

"It was a choice between one of these
or a dozen skimpy little roses."

"Dropping out of school
never done me no harm."

"I've still got a few
wrinkles to iron out."

"I used to have a dog, but he wouldn't eat my wife's leftovers."

"Miss Stokes, I've been looking at your work record, and you're taking far too many days off."

"I don't want that stuck right in front of the TV."

"You still having trouble sleeping?"

"What's the matter with you? That's the third time you've knocked over the coffee."

BEWARE OF 'LULU'

"He's down in the basement
cleaning the furnace."

"I thought we were supposed to go
on a world cruise when you retired."

"Anybody wanna cross the street?"

"Shouldn't be more than 10 minutes.
He was in a locker at the airport."

"Why did you move your plate?"

"According to the computer, we owe the
gas company $14.3 billion for August."

"Arnold, where can I lay my hands on a fan belt for a 1998 Cosmos Star cruiser?"

"If you don't mind me saying so, sir, he never did take well to captivity."

"Did I tell you I was voted 'The boy most likely to go somewhere'?"

"Of course I remembered your birthday! I had a drink with the guys at lunchtime."

"We had a trial separation, but she found me."

"Here's a nice two-bedroom apartment, but they don't allow pets."

". . . and cancel the tickets to Acapulco."

"It's a grocery list, Brother Clarence!"

"Here we are, Mount Everest.
I need 29,000 feet of rope."

"Dad, I've been thinking:
Why don't we get a dog?"

"Open the door. How can new
seat covers catch measles?"

"Your bank manager says he doesn't recommend surgery at this time."

"Bill specializes in the study of rare diseases."

"Have you done the north slope?"

"Did they tell you I had to take one of my pills at 2 o'clock?"

"So I said, 'If you want to do something useful around here, why don't you paint the fence?'"

"I wo
but

"I thought your résumé said
you did 40 words a minute."

"Can I drop you off somewhere?
I've decided to call a cab."

"Have any of you slaves
seen my sandwiches?"

"Did you say 'coffee and a bun'?"

"I'll have a glass
soda, and leave th

"I want you to ta
every six months
and see me next